DEEP WITHIN

TERESA COX BATES

A Molding Messengers Publication

Deep Within

Copyright © 2021 by Teresa Cox Bates

All rights reserved. Printed in the United States of America. No part of this book may be used or reproduced in any manner whatsoever without written permission of the publisher except in the case of brief quotations embodied in critical articles or reviews.

For information about permission to reproduce selections from this book, Write to:

Molding Messengers, LLC

1728 NE Miami Gardens Dr, Suite #111, North Miami Beach, FL, 33179

or email Info.Staff@MoldingMessengers.com.

www.MoldingMessengers.com

Library of Congress Control Number: 2021904349

Print ISBN: 978-0-578-87007-6

eBook ISBN: 978-0-578-87008-3

A Molding Messengers Publication

Author Biography

Teresa Cox-Bates was born and raised in Brooklyn, New York. She moved to Bellport in Long Island shortly after her father Reginald Cox passed away. Her mother Tracey Cox provided the very best for Teresa and her four siblings. Tiffany, Reggie, Robert, and Nate all grew up with many talents. Teresa married her college sweetheart John Bates. They have three beautiful children together Eli, Issac, and Ava Bates. Teresa's mentor Orin Dooling helped her to stay on the road to success. Teresa always put her heart into creating stories. A writer by day and a reader at night, Teresa pulls her inspiration from everything that she comes into contact with. Teresa's passion, energy, and drive, are true, real and undeniable. Teresa's passion is to help anyone that is in need. She dedicates her time and energy in helping to shape the world into a better place. Through Teresa's writing, her wish is to inspire as many individuals as she can. She wants everyone to take action on reaching their goals. All you need is already inside of you. All you need to do is to dig *Deep Within* yourself to approach the life that you were always meant to have. Stay Fulfilled!

Acknowledgement

I would like to thank my husband, John Bates, who always shows me unconditional love. To my three children Eli, Isaac and Ava Bates- you all taught me how to be a better person on this earth. Everything I do is for you. I want you all to always know that anything is possible. I also wish to express my deep appreciation for all of my friends and family that show their continued support for me.

This book is dedicated to all that believe in themselves and want the best in life. Everything you ever need is born within you, all you have to do is dig *Deep Within* and pull it out. My hope for everyone that reads this book is that you will find your way in life and that you are continuously motivated to stay on the path to successfulness professionally and personal growth.

Contents

INTRODUCTION 1

STAYING MOTIVATED NO MATTER THE OBSTACLE 4

BRAVE – DEVELOP A BRAVE HEART 7

    Routine 12

    Show Up For Yourself 17

PERSPECTIVE 29

    Change Your Perspective, Change Your Life! 31

SELF CONFIDENCE 37

    Do I Need To Be Confident? 38

    Building Confidence 39

    Benefits Of Self-Confidence 40

    Tips For Improving Your Self-Confidence 42

IDENTIFY YOUR PATH 44

    How To Find Your Path In Life 45

TIMING 48

    How To Trust The Timing Of Your Life 49

CONCLUSION 51

DEEP WITHIN

TERESA COX BATES

A Molding Messengers Publication

INTRODUCTION

Often, we hit midlife and discover that we have been functioning rather than living. We have found ways to meet the demands of everyday life, and we have often moved far beyond reasonable limits. We go on and on long after we feel the urge to stop, constantly ignoring our body's warning signs, usually until it's too late.

Our journals are often filled with things to do rather than filled with caring for ourselves and self-loving activities. If we don't take the time to take care of ourselves and our own well-being, we can become exhausted and irritable, and the result is that we don't pay attention to the things that really deserve our attention.

One of the most loving things we can do for ourselves is make time for ourselves. We often spend a lot of time caring for others, but we are not concerned with our own needs.

It's not uncommon in our busy, fast-paced, and multitasking world for people to simply run out of energy long before the end of a typical day. Not only do we constantly multitask and get bombarded with over thousands of sights and sounds every day, but our days are filled with the things we have to do, the things we do for others, and the things we should do for ourselves. The last thing on our list has always been to take care of ourselves.

Taking care of yourself should be the first on your daily "will do" list, not the last thing you tend to do only when you have time and energy to do it. Only by taking care of yourself first can you perform well at work, take good care of children, support your spouse, have equal relationships, or be a good volunteer.

Let's face it, if you can't love yourself, how can you embrace someone else's love?

You may feel unworthy of yourself, but you will still long for someone else's love. This is where the conflict arises. When you love yourself, life takes care of the details because everything else is minor compared to self-acceptance. Of course, there are times when you don't feel accepted and/or loved. This is normal and we all experience these moments. But self-acceptance is the foundation of a fulfilling life when you start to show up with your whole self.

Taking care of yourself is not the same as being selfish, but a new way of living life. Making self-care a priority will give you a more energetic way of living and thinking. Taking care of yourself mainly creates new and positive energy habits that reward you with productivity and efficiency during the day and with enough energy at the end of the day to perform other necessary tasks, enjoy your family and social participation and many more. Taking care of yourself first also creates a much less stressful environment.

While there are no magic cures when it comes to reducing stress in our lives and energizing self, there are a few simple steps you can follow that will help energize you and keep you going while reducing some of that stress in your world.

STAYING MOTIVATED NO MATTER THE OBSTACLE

Motivation involves strong mental power. It is believed that anything can be accomplished using the tools of the mind! It involves positive thinking and the willingness to motivate yourself toward a goal. In the course of your life you will have many goals to aspire and challenges to overcome. It is important that you stay motivated in order to enjoy life to the fullest!

Motivation can lead a person to success, and inner motivation is crucial to being optimistic about life. Since everyone is different, self help to motivation also varies and it is dependent upon priorities, as what motivates you may not pique another person's interest. Motivation is not easy because sometimes, it is difficult to identify it in yourself and the requirements you want in life. However, presenting the facts and taking charge of the reins is the right mindset to increase motivation.

Positive mindset is one of the key elements to keep you motivated. This tool can be used in all situations. It is common to think negatively about problems or challenges. This is usually the first thing that comes to mind, making it difficult to think positive. However, when faced with a problem, immediately find something positive about it. Although, it may be a small thing, but find it and focus on it. One way to avoid negative thoughts is to replace bad thoughts with good ones.

Something very important for motivation is maintaining a good level of self-worth (believing in yourself and your abilities without setting artificial limits). Having self-worth improves your potential is the right way to motivate yourself. Motivated people always ensure determination is stronger than their want to give up. They are less likely to be distracted by discouragement or minor difficulties along the way.

Self-motivation is based on feeling good and increasing self-esteem. These are some of the critical components that are contained in each person and the important point is to take the time to look within and unleash your potential. For a happy and successful life, motivation is imperative. Success is achieved by knowing your desires, like what and how you want things in life, and this leads to motivation. Also, being around positive people who really care about you and love you is very important. Having a negative environment will surely damage performance and loosen control of motivation.

Positive mindset and thinking can be used in all areas of life. Just replace the negative with a positive one. To motivate yourself for something you want to do, keep it small at first. It's also not a bad idea to reward yourself for staying motivated. Motivation can be achieved and conquered, it all depends on what you think and feel.

Remember, motivation is to face any obstacle and consistently be in action, no matter how small. Never giving up is the surest way to keep your head strong and move in the direction you want. Such motivation will never let you down and it all depends on your attitude. Staying motivated and positive at all times is difficult, but with personal support, the motivation would come easy.

BRAVE – DEVELOP A BRAVE HEART

I literally stumbled across life and gave my family many opportunities to laugh; and while the fall can be quite painful at times, thank goodness I am able to look at it and learn how to handle the potential for falls in the future.

To develop a courageous heart, you should consider the following:

- Agree never to be a candidate for downhill skiing
- Move slowly
- Stay focused
- And above all, laugh when it happens

One guarantee in life is that just as sure as you experience high points, you will surely fall too. The fall may not be in a physical sense, but more in a psychological sense there will betimes where. You're going to try something and it won't go as planned. We call it a mistake, a failure, a fiasco, or a disaster. It is good to know that unless one falls off a cliff into an abyss, we are likely to recover from a physical fall. But the psychological fall, well, that's a little more challenging to bounce back from.

A hit to the ego can cause lifelong pain and suffering and may prevent you from trying again. Over the years, I have developed techniques to overcome the possible chaos, shame, heartbreak, and debilitating fear that could come with a psychological downfall so that I am able to accept that in life I will keep making mistakes. I am not absolutely immune from these feelings coming back to me, but I am much more resilient and I will not let that stop me from trying again. To overcome the reluctance and fear of kicking myself, I developed a brave heart. My courage has gradually increased over time. When I was younger I never did anything spirited. I never did anything I wasn't good at, and since I didn't think I was good at anything, you get the idea. I never put myself in a position to suffer public embarrassment. I never laughed when I fell. I just wanted to crawl into a hole and never get out.

So, how did I transform from a shy, never take a chance because I am such a failure at everything kind of girl into a woman who says she has a brave heart? I'll tell you how I got it and you can have one too. Just think about the word B-R-A-V-E and change the internal label.

Internally brand yourself. We all have these little voices in our heads and some are louder than others. We often unconsciously identify ourselves through our internal dialogue. There is ample evidence that language influences the way we think. Remember: "We are what we think about all day." Replace any negative talk or language in your head with positive language. Do you remember the words I used to describe a psychological downfall - failure, mistake, fiasco, disaster? The way you label the "fall" will influence whether you try again.

For example, if you replace the word failure with lesson, you are more likely not to give up, whereas, if you use the word disaster as a description, that is when you crawl into a hole and never come out.

The word failure gets a bit tricky, as there is also a difference between calling something that you did a failure and calling yourself a failure. Be careful how you talk about yourself. Calling yourself a failure can turn into a self-fulfilling prophecy.

Developing a positive self image and a brave heart starts with what you have in your mind! Repeat. Even when you doubt yourself because sometimes, you don't really know what you are capable of until you try. If you want to dance, put on your dancing shoes. If you want to run, put on your running shoes. You can start by walking, but you will have the right shoes when you are ready to pick up the pace.

The more you say out loud and practice a new idea or behavior on your own, the more likely it is to become second nature. Don't worry if your partner or family sees you exercising in front of the bathroom mirror. Also, let them know that you are ready to be criticized and that you will not get defensive. Now is the time to have an open mind and accept whatever it is that is coming your way.

Also, be make sure there are positive people who will pump you up. You don't have to be famous to have a fan club. Accept what you can control and dive in when you know that you will do the best you can, but know that you are not always responsible for the outcome. Most of the time the outcome is out of your hands, but you can still celebrate your personal efforts because that is all you have control over. Your lists, plans, and actions are under your control and that is powerful. If things don't go exactly as planned, there still may be a lesson to be learned and an opportunity for growth. Remember, not getting what you want is sometimes a wonderful stroke of luck.

ARE YOU TOO SCARED TO IMPROVE?

It's okay to be afraid. Taking action and exposing yourself to everything that you fear or have been avoiding will give you a reward. Yes, you will feel some of those bad feelings that I mentioned as fear, but you will also feel better and have more energy and maybe even be proud of yourself.

Over time, the bad feelings go away and are replaced by more positive feelings. I can't tell you it's easy because I would lying, but I can tell you it will be worth it. Be brave and face what has set you back. Accept the *fact* when you are out of your comfort zone. You will feel uncomfortable, scared or apprehensive.

If you are faced with this feeling, no matter what goal you choose, you will be successful. The process is a bit twisted. If you live in your comfort zone all the time, you will eventually feel uncomfortable and if you live outside your comfort zone, eventually you will feel good. So be brave and strong, get out of your comfort zone.

PREPARE YOURSELF EMOTIONALLY

It can be difficult to fully prepare emotionally for what will happen if plans or actions do not go as planned. But it helps if you can imagine possible scenarios and how you will cope with yourself. Write down your coping strategies so you can refer to them when you are not thinking clearly. Knowing that you have a fallback, emotional support from your fan club, and future opportunities to try again can lessen the impact if you don't get the ideal result. And give yourself time to process, whether it's ideal or not. Take time for solitude and reflection.

It takes only one second to be brave. To fight the good fight. I know that every day isn't all peaches and roses, but that's when the growth happens. We can't always be comfortable in our lives, in these moments being uncomfortable determines how we will gain character. If the walk is always hard then you are doing something right. Nothing ever comes easy. If you want it you must work for it. You can gain muscle if you never pick up the weights. Stop having pity parties complaining and murmuring about what hasn't happened yet because it is obvious that it's not the time and place for you.

ROUTINE

We often overestimate what we can do in a year and drastically underestimate how much we can do in a decade. If you are not achieving all of the goals you set for yourself from the beginning, this is definitely not the time to give up, but rather to look at your long-term goals. Fail every day, stay focused, and review the actions you've taken, are you getting the results you want? If not then, you should have the courage to review and improve your daily actions and routines.

You need to make a habit, that is, a daily routine. A routine is an efficient way to use your time as it guides you through your actions. You know when to wake up, what to do when you wake up, how you want your day to go, and when your day eventually ends.

If you are a bit disappointed in your results so far, you are certainly not alone. Setting goals to achieve goals is an art and the result of developing a set of successful habits that will aid in your efforts to achieve your goals. If your daily actions and routines don't support you on your way to achieving your goal, you will continue to spin your wheels and remain frustrated with your progress.

The first thing you must learn to win a war is urgency. If you spend most of your day chasing your own tail and can't focus on your priorities, you can't take the actions you need to achieve your goals. Regain control of your life today and start a new routine by planning your day the day before. This simple change allows you to be in control of your day immediately instead of your day controlling you.

If you plan your day the night before, you will wake up each day with a clear plan of what you will accomplish and well-defined windows of time when you will achieve it. When planning your day the night before, set aside time each day to work on priorities specific to your goal. That little change in creating new habits that requires planning your day and planning the time to reach your main goals for the day will set you up for success.

When you are living in a modality of constant overwhelm and urgency, you are constantly distracted. Your attention is focused on putting fires out, instead of carrying out goal achieving activities. Your challenge and the reason you have achieved very little in terms of your goals is not due to time starvation, it is simply that you have not scheduled time in your day to carry out your priorities. You are, in essence, allowing what appear to be urgent tasks, to crowd out your goal and priorities, because you are not in control of your time.

Yes, we do encounter deadlines and fires that we need to put out from time to time, but if fires and crisis are the norm in your life, now is the time to assess how you are handling things in your life. Are you so lost in the crisis management wormhole that you have lost sight of the big picture? If you're feeling this way, it's definitely time for you to take a break as soon as possible to reconsider how you're doing. When you get back the rein of control and your routines and habits support your success, you empower yourself to be the manager of your day and make sure you take your time and meet your specific priorities each day.

Urgent matters will always still require your attention, time and energy, but you will understand that your efforts to achieve your goals will not place the same strict demands on you. They are critical to our success and must be given the priority they deserve every day. If you continue to do what you have done in the past, you will definitely continue to get the same results. For better results in achieving your goals, stop authorizing urgent tasks immediately to prevent you from reaching your daily priorities. The challenge you face is that the specific priorities of your goals do not place such high demands on you. So you prioritize them lower every day. As long as you continue to give low priority each day to achieving your specific priorities for your goals, you will continue to make mistakes in life and will never achieve your goals and dreams.

Ideally, everyone has a routine, but most of us don't have a daily routine that fits our long-term goals.

IDENTIFY YOUR LONG-TERM GOALS

Where do you want to be in 3, 5 or 10 years? There are two ways to get to a destination. You can choose a destination and create plans, or you can walk away and hope to eventually find yourself at your destination. Obviously, the first option is better. It is best to start a trip with an eye toward your destination. Your daily routine should bring you closer to your goal - your dream for the future.

CREATE A DAILY ROUTINE THAT FOCUSES ON YOUR GOALS.

You cannot achieve your goals overnight, therefore, you need to break them down into milestones - manageable items and set daily tasks that will bring you closer to your final goal. Remember that a daily routine does not have to be the same actions every day, however, you should plan for it a week in advance. A good plan would be to plan the entire week. Pick a day to complete this task. Most people choose Sunday afternoons to be able to look at the week ahead.

CONSIDER YOUR ENERGY LEVELS WHEN PLANNING YOUR DAYS

First, make a list of the tasks you want to do each day of the week. Don't omit anything, no matter how mundane it sounds. Now look at your energy levels - when are you most productive? The idea is to distribute the demanding tasks when you are most energetic.

ESTABLISH A DAILY RITUAL

A ritual brings rhythm and pleasure into your life. A good morning ritual is an activity that brings positivity. It could be reading a favorite blog or listening to an inspiring podcast. Other rituals that should be part of your routine - morning or evening include:

- Exercise and eat healthy food
- Meditate
- Take breaks at the right time
- Sleep well
- Have time for your family

A morning routine is especially important. You should start the day right by doing something that will increase your energy levels, improve your mental focus, and stimulate your creativity.

STICK TO THE PLAN

All planning is in vain if you don't stick to routine. Sticking to the routine will be difficult at first as old habits and routines will have to be eliminated. However, if you continue your new routine sporadically, it will take longer for it to stick.

EVALUATE YOUR ROUTINE

Is your new routine working? If it isn't, you have to change it.

You can start with a 30-day evaluation. After 30 days, identify the challenges and motivations for your new routine. Eliminate tasks that don't help your end goal. If your routine isn't the problem, find out what went wrong and plan how not to fail. The most important thing is to establish a habit that contributes to your ultimate goal.

SHOW UP FOR YOURSELF

You never really thought that you will find yourself in this place at this time. You may ask yourself, what am I doing here? How did I get to this place? And the most important question is how do you get out of this space? There may be an area that you've been trying to escape for a very long time and it seems like the walls keep rising as you continue crying more desperately seeking answers for the solutions you yearn for. When all these things are happening, who do you turn to? What is the most important aspect of your life that keeps you going? The motivation that always keeps the fire going?

Sometimes, the fire goes out and then we have to figure out how to light it again. We ask ourselves, is it worth living again? Do we need to have a fire at all? On the days where this is the self-sabotaging image that you face, in that moment is the time that you have to show up for yourself.

Showing up for yourself means that you have to put in the work to get on the path that you want to be and not looking for someone else to do it for you but you find it within yourself to do it for yourself. And by doing all of these things that occurs for your fire to continue, start off little and grow rapidly. Although, it may burn you a bit in the beginning because you're so shocked but going far, you will feel like a brand new person, you will feel like you are on top of the world, you will feel like nothing can stop you. Those are the days where what you have been working on. On these days, things like the projects that you've been faced with now get much easier for you.

It is much easier to show up for somebody else than it is for yourself. Many people don't show up for themselves they always reach out for others. They always look for the comfort and approval of others, however, there are times in life you need to show up for yourself.

You need to show up for you because no one else is going to do it for you. No one else is going to put in the work like you do. For example, like setting a goal and sticking to it. I know it's cliché to use the example of going to the gym to lose weight to get healthy, but I will say this, when you set goals for yourself and put yourself in the path of staying focus on that which you want. To get out of life, ask yourself what is it that you want to succeed in? And what is that you want to project onto others now going to the gym? Is it working out or eating right?

There are so many ways to show up for yourself, but unfortunately, there are more distractions and ways to ignore your needs and not show up for yourself! To some, showing up means sticking to your meditation program, or taking advantage of your routine, or doing your new exercise routine, or expressing your feelings instead of stuffing them down and exploding at a later time.

Be honest, have you been showing up for yourself recently? And if not, why? You may not show up for yourself because:

- You may feel guilty if you put yourself first
- You may be afraid that when you show up for yourself, people will see you as being selfish
- You may still think that your focus should be to take care of everyone

Let's be clear, I'm not talking about being selfish. That is completely different. I mean to show up for yourself in a healthy and regular way so that in turn you can be present and show up for others in a healthy way. And if you're not showing up for yourself, what are you going to change in your life or your schedule so that you can start doing so?

This is very important because if you don't show up for yourself, you will indirectly teach others how to treat and interact with you. The needs of others are always different and when you are not used to taking care of yourself in whatever ways work for you, it becomes too easy to continue to ignore your own needs.

When you ignore your needs, you won't be able to "be there" for your family, pets, or friends, you can't be a good listener, and you can't offer comfort, solace, or love if you don't first show up for yourself. For instance, showing up regularly for myself helps me to renew my commitment every 3-6 months. These days I meditate, tap in, and do a new form of healing every day no matter what. That is how I have to do it because I know that if I skip a day, I will easily skip a week and before I know it, the wheels have come off! The good news is, however, that I know what I need and I know that only I can meet those needs.

So the question is, are you really ready to show up for yourself?

Why don't you want to show up for yourself? Because often when you do, your life and relationships improve, you take better care of your health, you share your feelings more openly, and you experience more joy

When you are ready to show up for yourself, the universe hears that you intend to take care of yourself and improve your life. And when you tell the universe that you are ready to respect who you are and what your needs are, the universe will help you by showing up for you too.

When you are ready to show up for yourself, you will release the resistance in your energy field and start to notice how much abundance there is in your life. When you Show Up For Yourself, it clarifies the energy of desire in your life and the universe will assist you in surprising new ways by opening up new channels of abundance.

WHY IS IT IMPORTANT TO SHOW UP FOR YOURSELF?

Showing up for yourself is important simply because YOU ARE IMPORTANT. As we all know for sure that, you are a person on this earth, living your one and only life just like all beings everywhere who want to be happy, fulfilled, and fully alive. Showing up for yourself is the foundation to this important work. As a person on this earth, you deserve to be nurtured, nourished and supported by the most important person, YOU.

You may think that you can get away with it without showing up for yourself. And yes, that is technically correct. You *can* get away with it. You can survive, you can languish, but you want more than that, you want to flourish and prosper, to live as your full and great fulfillment.

To show up for yourself with joy and authenticity to others in service, you must also nourish yourself. We cannot pour from an empty cup. Trying to be of service out of self-sacrifice is unsustainable. We burn out. No one is served by our burning out, not in the long-term, anyway.

SOME WAYS TO SHOW UP FOR YOURSELF EVERY DAY

Sometimes when our plates are full of plans, deadlines, commitments and expectations, our subconscious mind plays a trick on us, and this can happen especially if you are wondering about stretching yourself thin. In other words, if you ask your brain to operate on all cylinders, the chatter to stop yourself can get very loud.

Showing up for yourself means being really alive, affirming yourself. To understand what this means, let's think otherwise – the opposite of showing up for yourself - by saying no to yourself. The feeling behind you saying NO to yourself is being numb to your desires and your goals. This is where your brain plays tricks on you, numbing you out with activities that stop the yes. Just picture it as those nasty little scrubbing bubbles that come in and wipe everything out

How do you numb yourself out? The numbing is removing your mind from the present moment, from being fully alive in your body, and from the circumstance you want to be focusing on. Numbing activities could include surfing the Internet, watching television, over sleeping, eating when you're not hungry, drinking, or burying yourself in frivolous activities. They can be addictive, so acknowledgment is the first step.

Tools To Use To Show Up For Yourself Every Day

Awareness

Be on the lookout when you start to venture into numbing activities or when you hear yourself say, "Tomorrow is another day," which means you are putting off for tomorrow what you can do today.

Get Fully Involved By Anchoring Yourself In The Room

Recognize the objects around you, feel your body in your chair, feel the texture of your clothes, notice the tapping of your fingers on the computer keys, the pressure of the pen against your middle joint, the grain of the wood on the desk in front of you. Being present – showing up for yourself, can discourage you from engaging in numbing activities.

Use Your Breath

Connect with your breathing by pausing to take ten deep breaths. Get out if you can. Breathing in nature can be a good way to illuminate your mind.

Get Physical

Regular exercises increase dopamine in your brain, increasing its ability to absorb and process information.

Some inspirational quotes to encourage you to show up and take care of yourself

1. "You yourself, as much as anybody in the entire universe deserves your love and affection." – Budda
2. "Self-Care has very little to do with your outer self. It's about accepting all of yourself." – Tyra Banks
3. "Self-care is never a selfish act – it is simply stewardship of the only gift I have, the gift I was put on earth to offer to others." – Parker Palmer
4. "Before anything else or anyone else, make sure you're taking care of yourself. If you're not treating yourself well on the inside, you will not be happy or healthy on the outside. Self-care is essential to your wellness." – Unknown
5. "Your time is limited, so don't waste it living someone else's life. Don't be trapped by dogma — which is living with the results of other people's thinking. Don't let the noise of others' opinions drown out your own inner voice. And most importantly, have the courage to follow your heart and intuition. They somehow

already know what you truly want to become. Everything else is secondary." – Steve Jobs

6. "Each time a woman stands up for herself, without knowing it possibly, without claiming it, she stands up for all women." – Maya Angelou

7. "When I loved myself enough, I began leaving whatever wasn't healthy. This meant people, jobs, my own beliefs, and habits – anything that kept me small, judgment called it disloyal. Now I see it as self-loving." – Kim McMilllen

8. "If you celebrate your differentness, the world will, too. It believes exactly what you tell it—through the words you use to describe yourself, the actions you take to care for yourself, and the choices you make to express yourself. Tell the world you are one-of-a-kind creation who came here to experience wonder and spread joy. Expect to be accommodated." – Victoria Moran

9. "Love yourself first, and everything else falls in line. You really have to love yourself to get anything done in this world." – Lucille Ball

10. "The best day of your life is the one on which you decide your life is your own. No apologies or excuses. No one to lean on, rely on, or blame. The gift is yours – it is an amazing journey – and you alone are responsible for the quality of it. This is the day your life really begins." – Bob Moawad

11. "I have come to believe that caring for myself is not self-indulgent. Caring for myself is an act of survival." – Audre Lorde
12. "Self-care is giving the world the best of you, instead of what's left of you." — Katie Reed
13. "When you say 'yes' to others make sure you are not saying 'no' to yourself." — Paulo Coelho
14. "As you grow older, you will discover that you have two hands, one for helping yourself, the other for helping others." — Maya Angelou
15. "With every act of self-care your authentic self gets stronger, and the critical, fearful mind gets weaker. Every act of self-care is a powerful declaration: I am on my side, I am on my side, each day I am more and more on my own side." – Susan Weiss Berry
16. "It's not selfish to love yourself, take care of yourself, and to make your happiness a priority. It's necessary." – Mandy Hale
17. "When you recover or discover something that nourishes your soul and brings joy, care enough about yourself to make room for it in your life." – Jean Shinoda Bolen
18. "I believe that the greatest gift you can give your family and the world is a healthy you." – Joyce Meyer
19. "Nourishing yourself in a way that helps you blossom in the direction you want to go is attainable, and you are worth the effort." – Deborah Day

20. "You can't hate yourself happy. You can't criticize yourself thin. You can't shame yourself worthy. Real change begins with self-love and self-care." – Jessica Ortner
21. "Compassionate action has to start with ourselves. If we are willing to stand fully in our own shoes and never give up on ourselves, then we will be able to put ourselves in the shoes of others and never give up on them." – Pema Chodron
22. "The journey isn't about becoming a different person. It's about loving who you are right now." – Suzanne Heyn
23. "If your compassion does not include yourself, it is incomplete." – Buddha
24. "How you love yourself is how you teach others to love you." – Rupi Kaur
25. "Be the very love that you crave." – Christine Kane
26. "Loving yourself isn't vanity; it's sanity." – Katrina Mayer
27. "I think the reward for conformity is that everyone likes you except yourself." – Rita Mae Brown
28. "When a woman becomes her own best friend life is easier." – Diane Von Furstenberg
29. "One of the greatest regrets in life is being what others would want you to be, rather than being yourself." – Shannon L. Alder
30. "When you stop living your life based on what others think of, your real life begins. At that moment, you will finally see the door of self-acceptance opened." – Shannon Adler

31. "Lighten up on yourself. No one is perfect. Gently accept your humanness." – Deborah Day
32. "You'll never know who you are unless you shed who you pretend to be." – Vironika Tugaleva
33. "The most powerful relationship you will ever have is the relationship with yourself." – Steve Maraboli
34. "Beauty begins the moment you decide to be yourself." – Coco Chanel

PERSPECTIVE

As I sit down to write these words, tears roll down my face. It feels good to start the emotions so I can put things in perspective. There was a time when my mind definitely clouded my judgment. The intense and uninterrupted thoughts of life weighed on me like a ship's anchor. I felt stagnant and lost. My world as I knew it was falling apart. Walls collapsing, windows breaking, and doors busted. I was inundated with the emotional bearings I was carrying. I just couldn't do it anymore. My weakness was that I couldn't be weak. I always thought that if I took a strong stance, everything would be fine. The truth is that it made things much worse. Suddenly I would burst into tears out of the blue. I wanted to sleep, I didn't want to eat, and despite how bad it was, my daily routine was interrupted, which made me not take care of myself.

There is a well-known saying: "It is not what happens to you, but the importance and meaning you give to what happens to you that matters most." This shows in many lives. In some cases, it may be a little forgotten or overlooked detail. In other areas, interpreting an experience fueled by deep emotions can affect how one sees life as warm and caring, while another sees it cold and overwhelming.

Our thoughts influence the way we perceive our world and create our reality. The way we perceive things is our perspective, our perspective influences every movement we make in our life.

Every negative thought or expression we put into the world limits and ultimately defeats us. We convince ourselves that we simply cannot move forward or that we lack fulfillment in our lives. While we have an absolute right to the things we create, we sometimes take an injustice perspective when we don't get what we want right away; this creates an overindulged attitude of entitlement which then convinces us that we will always lose even before we try. So we yell, "This is so unjust!" or "That's not fair!"

Without the development of a proper perspective, the variations in interpretations that influence counterproductive behavior can linger throughout a person's lifespan. The belief becomes a self-fulfilling prophecy. Reality supports this truth; we don't see the world as it is, but as we are. *As a man or woman thinks, so is he or she,* therefore, it is vital to develop and maintain a proper perspective on the quality of life you are experiencing.

CHANGE YOUR PERSPECTIVE, CHANGE YOUR LIFE!

Our thoughts, minds, and perspective are very powerful. If we pay attention to our thoughts, even the simplest ones, and connect, we can change and improve our whole lives! A small change in perspective can make a difference. We have several options every day to choose our perspective. It's like choosing which pair of sunglasses we want to look through. We have the option of being negative or positive. We get the opportunity to see another person's point of view. We can expand our minds and see things differently. We get to loosen our grip a bit on life so we can enjoy more.

For you, a perspective is a belief or truth of something that you have believed in for years.

For example, if you've always told people that you don't like rain, then this is a belief for you. This may be true for a number of reasons, but what if you could erase that suffocating thought and replace it with a new one? You could even create a new experience to change your perspective. Instead of always concentrating on everything you don't like about the rain, think of all the reasons to love the rain; the sound is soothing and calming, it smells good, you want to curl up on the couch and read a book when it rains, it helps clean your driveway, cultivate your garden, etc. Maybe next time it rains, you will go out without an umbrella and dance and jump in puddles to bring out your inner child act!

Life constantly presents situations to you that allow you to evaluate your perspective and change it to a healthier one.

Changing Our Perspective Helps Us Feel More Grateful

Changing our minds and perspectives towards healthier ones applies to everything. Changing your perspective for a while can help you connect more deeply with others, be more compassionate, have a deeper sense of gratitude, and become a more whole person. When you realize that by changing your perspective, big things can be seen as small things, it then becomes much more difficult to worry about anything.

Let's take action and pay attention to our thoughts and perspectives. Let's open our minds to see the other side. Let's make small changes that make us feel better and more positive. Let's look at different points of view and dig our heels into the sand. Let's imagine we're on vacation and appreciate the things we take for granted and seeing things with new eyes! Which pair of sunglasses will you wear today? Change your perspective and finally your life!

Assumptions - Proper Perspective

To develop a proper perspective towards yourself and your life, you must first question the assumptions you have about life. Why? Because your assumptions are the root of your perceptions and your perceptions are the lens through which you view yourself and the world. If your assumptions about yourself and life are the result of limited perceptions influenced by the social conditioning of people, environments and experiences, you are approaching life with a limited or scarcity mindset.

On the other hand, if your assumptions about life and yourself are the result of a broad vision influenced by the social conditioning that you have experienced of people, environments and experiences, you will approach life with a mindset of expansion or abundance. .

Our social status influences our assumptions about life. If our assumptions are not challenged, each of us could live our entire lives based on the thoughts and beliefs of others. It is sad, but true for many people. Only when we are exposed to new ways of thinking do we look at a different perspective on a particular thing. Very few people think about what they think and why.

It Is The Best For You

To develop a proper perspective on life, you need to think about how you are processing or filtering information from your experience and why you are interpreting the experience the way you are. Once you are aware of the root of an assumption, you can root out any social wiring that creates a particular mental script that no longer serves the best interests of your current goals and aspirations.

How It Creates Added Value

Developing the proper perspective to life adds value to your life in several ways. Some of these benefits are as follows:

- A proper perspective influences your attitudes and behaviors. Regardless of whether or not your perspective has been influenced by "seeing" life with a poor or abundant mindset, one thing is for sure; you think, feel, and act in accordance with the most dominant emotional thoughts and patterns.
- A proper perspective bestows light on and helps you see when your perspective on life is based on limited point of view.
- A proper perspective allows you to establish personal values based on principles that never change and are not subjective to changing realities.
- Proper perspective helps you recognize how the way you see a problem can actually be the problem. Einstein said, "The significant problem we face cannot be solved at the same level of thinking we were at when we created them."

- A good perspective allows you to listen to and respect other people's perspectives, even if they differ from your own.
- A proper perspective has the power to unleash the divine potential within you. It helps your ability to push boundaries as you expand your vision and life territory.
- A proper perspective gives you the mental toughness to overcome challenges and not let a temporary circumstance determine a permanent state of mind and life.
- A proper perspective recognizes that changes are made first from the inside out. We often pray and hope that the situation will change. Usually, it is a change in our view of the situation that prompts us to take the necessary steps to change the situation.

From now on, you have the option to decide for yourself how you would like to perceive your situation, an opportunity that you have before you, or a challenge or a goal that you face. The choice is yours to change your perspective.

A magnet has a negative side and a positive side. We are very similar to magnets, if we perceive our world in a positive way, obviously we will naturally attract positive outcomes. And likewise, if we perceive our life and world in a negative way, reverse is the case. Choose a perspective in which you focus on the tremendous blessings you have in life and the blessings you have bestowed on yourself. Why look the other way? It will only deter you from the result you want to achieve. Remember, Positive Perspective - Positive Outcomes!

SELF CONFIDENCE

Self-confidence is an inner feeling of absolute certainty about yourself and your own abilities. It is a psychological and social idea based on your confidence and belief in your own abilities, judgment and power. It is believing in your ability to deal with life no matter what it throws at you. It is also often equated with courage, although they are not exactly the same. There are elements of courage and self-esteem that you can gain in your way of learning to be confident. Courage helps build confidence because it is about dealing with fear, while ironically confidence can initially describe a lack of fear to begin with. Self-esteem focuses on the magnitude with which you are able to view yourself in a favorable way. In short, self-esteem can most easily be described as "how much you love yourself," and that's a big part of your self-confidence too. Although they are not the same, the terms "self-confidence" and "self-esteem" are often used interchangeably. Learning to be confident will undoubtedly involve elements of courage and self-esteem.

Self-confidence is the knowledge and understanding you have about certain talents and strengths. It is the awareness of what you can do and the desire to do the best you can with excellence. Real confidence does not mean that you are better than others, it means knowing that there are things you can do better than anyone else.

Where some think you have to have a big ego to be confident, the truth is that true self-confidence is humble and focused. Someone who possesses real confidence will do things very well and will not feel the need to let everyone know they did it. Excellence is always recognized by those who see it. It is the person who lacks confidence that feels compelled to tell everyone around what they did or are doing.

Being confident means knowing that you can be successful in certain areas of life. You also realize that others also have strengths and are better than you in certain areas. This awareness is not a threat to the confident person, but it is celebrated. Just as they want to do their best, they are happy in seeing others do their best as well. It is a lack of confidence that makes a person feel threatened by the success of others. Lack of self-confidence makes people feel like they are always competing with another to be the best. If they are not considered the best in everything; they get angry, they get depressed and cruel.

DO I NEED TO BE CONFIDENT?

When you feel confident, you have the courage to step up and face the challenges that await you. Self-confidence is knowing that you are capable of achieving your goals. It is knowing that even if you fail in this attempt, you learn from your mistakes, move forward and in the end, you win. Confident people are those who develop the determination to carry on even in the face of great difficulties.

Self-confidence gives us courage and helps us to think clearly and correctly. You don't have to spend countless hours wondering what you are going to do or if you can do it. Self-confidence is not about "if", but about "when". When a person thinks about when to have their opportunity or when to face it, they are prepared and ready for it. They will think about it every day and will always be aware of what is happening in their life so as not to miss anything. Self-confidence prepares us and when we feel prepared, we feel confident. You can see how everything builds on itself and makes you stronger and stronger.

BUILDING CONFIDENCE

Having understood a little what self-confidence is and what is not; let's talk about how we can develop self-confidence in our lives. Some people have a greater capacity to build confidence than others. There are people whose style of behavior tends to be more confident and whose nature is to build their confidence without much concentration or effort. I also believe that there are people who find it very difficult to develop self-confidence in all areas of life. They are naturally shy, withdrawn, and don't really believe in their abilities. However, it is possible and necessary for each person to work on their level of confidence in order to achieve the focus of their desires.

Self-confidence is an emotional force and therefore must be controlled and used. The same goes for anger, love, hatred, passion, worry, and other emotions that can cause us great harm if left unchecked. At the same time, we cannot live in our life without these emotions. They are like fire; when used and controlled: fire provides heat, cooks food, generates energy, and more. Out of control and misused, fire is one of the most destructive forces on the planet. Fire destroys cities, claims countless lives and leave total destruction in its path. Self-confidence that is not controlled and abused leads to selfishness, pride, and emotional destruction. Controlled and properly used self-confidence will lead to success, service, and life satisfaction.

BENEFITS OF SELF-CONFIDENCE

Take a look around and you can easily spot someone who lacks self-confidence. You can tell the difference between one who behaves with confidence and one who is shy and fearful. Self-confidence shows the physical appearance of a person. A person who stands tall and confident is likely to be a self-confident person. This is in contrast to a person who could barely hold his head up while walking due to his lack of confidence. Confidence in yourself definitely has advantages. In addition to being able to do whatever you want, a self-confident person can enjoy a variety of benefits including:

Improved Performance

Healthy self-confidence is enough for anyone whose life involves interacting with people to do the best they can. They recognize the essence of self-confidence to reach their peak performance and help them overcome the obstacles that stand in their way. For people who lack self-confidence, it is something that they really need to work on to be self-confident if they want to be successful.

Satisfaction And Happiness

Self-confident people are generally happier. They show satisfaction in their life compared to those who did not have that level of self-confidence. Ultimately, this leads to quality work, superior performance, better relationships, and a sense of agreement with the world. For most self-confident people, they feel that "nothing can go wrong" and if something did happen, they could handle it.

Social Comfort

Acceptance, recognition, and approval from society are all important to a person's existence. Those who are self-confident are only able to achieve these. Their belief in themselves makes them more relaxed in social situations. They are not afraid to be with other people and meet new people in any social setting. A good level of self-confidence leads to a high level of comfort in people, regardless of who is around them.

They are seen as excited about life and the future, which is reflected in their relationships with others. Their positive aura becomes a kind of magnet that draws people to them. Their enthusiasm is contagious and is passed on to the people around them.

Leadership Potential

What makes a good leader? Leadership comes from self-confidence. Without self-confidence, it would be difficult for anyone to lead, much less get others to follow them. Without a command, a person may have a difficult time convincing others of his/her leadership qualities and abilities. Self-confidence is the basic and fundamental quality of a good leader.

TIPS FOR IMPROVING YOUR SELF-CONFIDENCE

- Never allow anyone to bring you down.
- Be the best "YOU" you can be.
- Don't compare yourself to others.
- Don't bottle it up; let it go in some way.
- Taking care of yourself is the first step to feeling better and more confident in your life.

- You have talents, skills and abilities waiting to be developed and used.
- Find ways to incorporate the positive qualities you admire into your personality.
- Find current mentors, role models, and copy the person you admire, but don't betray who you are.
- Make step-by-step changes every day. It will lead you to a great transformation
- Meditate every day.
- Always be grateful.

IDENTIFY YOUR PATH

Every day is a day when you either walk your own path or a day when you walk a path that fate or someone else has chosen for you.

Time is the most precious commodity on earth. Once your time is up, that is all. You have to decide which path to follow and you have to start walking that path as quickly as possible.

No one path is straight and narrow. It has many ups and downs. I want to think of my journey as a staircase. I used to let the ebb and flow of life's tides take me where they wanted me to go. It was like a ship at sea without a captain at the helm, it was only a matter of time before I would end up shipwrecked on the rocks of life.

Fortunately, I was able to regain control of my life. I chose to be the captain of my fate. I decided to choose my own path and not let fate or some other outside influence decide my future for me. I knew I couldn't change my life overnight, but I knew I could get things going and take action to make my life go the path I wanted. I decided what I wanted to be, what I wanted to do and have in this life, and I began to take steps to make my dreams come true. When I decided what I wanted to be, do and have in life, everything became clear, scattered thought patterns disappeared, and I was extremely focused on what I wanted from life and how I would get it. I made small changes every day - consistent small changes. I surrounded myself with mentors and found the people who had achieved what I wanted to achieve. I took the path of least resistance and learned from their mistakes, which helped me get where I wanted to be faster than if I had to rely on trial and error.

If you discipline yourself to make constant small daily changes, I guarantee that you will get a lot more than you thought you would get. You would have chosen your own path and have started to follow it. And if you continue on your own path, within a few years you will no longer be able to recognize the person you have become.

HOW TO FIND YOUR PATH IN LIFE

To answer the question of how to find your path in life, I would first like to point out that it is different and more important to find your path in life than to find your purpose in life. When people talk about or explore their purpose in life, many of them have ideas about their purpose, but don't know where to start. Or other people make lists of passions, dos and don'ts, but they still cannot find their purpose. Or people question themselves "is this what I am supposed to be doing?".

And once you're ready to take action to find your purpose in life, FEAR is another big challenge most people face when making changes in life. For example, fear of making the wrong decision, fear of not being good enough, fear of failure, etc. This fear can lead to pain, shame, confusion, and of course we don't want that.

When you focus on finding your path in life, the mind is less focused on how things "should be" and on certain outcomes. You see, when you focus on your PURPOSE; you want it to be perfect, you want to be an expert in what you do, you want to work for the best company, you want to work with passion every day, but when you focus on how to find your PATH in life; then you are not focused on an outcome, so the barrier to change, the barrier to perfection and being good enough and accepted, is less difficult and challenging, there is less pressure and less fear. So there is less resistance to change.

If you focus on finding your path in life, over time your purpose will evolve and your purpose will be to find your path. This is the missing key that you are not told about.

There are basically 4 types of people who are looking to find their path in life. These people have different outlooks on life. They may say:

- I have no idea, never thought about it, I don't know, I don't care, the purpose and the way of life are completely absurd and wrong.
- I have heard about it, I am confused, lost and unsure. I want to find it, but I don't know how.

- I have taken steps to find my path and my purpose, but I still find it difficult. I don't know how to make the right decisions because I'm still not happy. Is this where I'm supposed to be?
- I am on my path in life and my purpose evolves as I get older. I contribute and give back without stopping to learn along the way of life.

In short, to find your path in life, you simply have to follow your heart and your intuition. When finding your path, don't use your mind, use your heart, be confident and faith in life. This is how you align your inner and outer self.

There are people who live their life only based on goals and expectations, that's not where you want to go. It's okay to be successful but if that's not in line with who you are; you will not be happy, you will burnout and feel lonely. You want to live a life true to yourself and that is to find YOUR way - the way of your heart, all you need to do is to learn to listen.

The journey of life is the journey towards self-realization. To fill that void, you need to fill the void between your outer world and your inner world, and finding your path is one way to do that.

TIMING

Sometimes we face challenges in life. While some days go by easily, others are a bit difficult. We can say don't worry about the little things and some opportunities that are easier said than done. We spend countless hours of our lives dealing with things we have no control over. We may be upset by what other people say or do, but we don't really have control over any of it. When you get upset, all you can do is what you can afford. If you have done all that you can, you should be at ease with that knowledge.

A mountain in a mole is a term I like to use. It just means that something can be so small, but when you are really stressed it becomes a big problem. Worrying takes a lot of time and energy and is not good for us. You have to learn to ignore the unimportant things in life. You have to learn to tune out the non-important things in life. You have to tune out non-important issues. You have to tune out all the negatives that will turn that mole hill into a mountain. Consider your time; worrying about things does not give you an answer any faster. Worrying will not change anything, it will cost you countless hours of unproductivity and this is no good for your health.

Trust who you are and your abilities. Be happy with who you are. Don't worry about negative external sources that don't lead you to a positive place. You don't have to worry about something someone said or a place someone else thinks you should be. You are in this moment and this moment will never happen again! Don't waste time worrying about something you have no control over. Take yourself to a higher level of thinking by not focusing on what you can or cannot be. It will happen the way it will, be prepared, but don't overindulge in countless hours and days of worrying. Don't let the things that you have no control over get you upset, focus on the positive.

HOW TO TRUST THE TIMING OF YOUR LIFE

Have you ever beat yourself up for not being where you think you should be? I know you have and many times in fact. Maybe you thought you'd be further along in your career. Or maybe you thought you'd be married and have kids at this stage of your life. Or maybe you thought you'd be more disciplined, fitter and happier by now.

The illusions about you and the world are one. Therefore, all forgiveness is a gift to you. Your goal is to discover who you are and clearly trust the universe. It means having confidence in where you are in your life, regardless of the landscape of your current reality.

Trust the timing of your life and try to see what happens without judgment. When you remove the judgment of "how you think things should be" and accept them for what they are, you remove all feelings of weakness, tension, and fatigue from your mind. It automatically frees you from guilt and shame. That doesn't mean you should stop having a great life for yourself, you should. This is just to say that by creating your life you can experience peace with the timing of it all.

Create Peace In Your Life By:

- Becoming aware of the thoughts that are automatic in your mind and changing them if necessary.
- React less to the things that trigger it.
- Create and maintain healthy boundaries with the people in your life.
- Supporting yourself in spiritual practice every day.

CONCLUSION

Setting goals make people more positive and motivated to work towards it and the moment one views success of accomplishing things in life as per the desire; they stay motivated to do more things. Self help to motivation has its main foundation in self believing, and having a low self-esteem affects the life negatively. Taking the lead and challenging it with full motivation is possible only when a person is prepared to accept help himself or herself. Similarly, to stay motivated read positive books as it assists in growing in leaps and bonds.

There are times when people feel like things are out of control, hopeless, and the spirit of motivation seems to fade. Now is the time to consider how to respond appropriately and energetically, which leads to the right path to motivation. Identify the positive concepts and identify the questions for yourself and begin to answer them. You will discover that this is a real way to motivate yourself in difficult situations. Recognize the dimly glowing hope, dig under it and identify the source of concern and face it with courage, self-confidence, and self-respect.

Make the decisive decision today not to let go of your ultimate goal of achieving priorities. These important matters that require your immediate attention in most cases are not your urgent problems, but someone else's urgent problem, and in most cases, they can wait an hour while you reach your specific priorities. As you use this new daily routine or habit to accomplish your specific priorities each day, you will be amazed at how many of your goals you can accomplish.

Regain control and let nothing less than a life and death situation to allow you to cancel a time for yourself. Free yourself from the tyranny of submitting to the will of these urgent tasks. You are responsible for your future – take charge of it, stop acting like an absenteeism owner over how things will turn out and actually carry out your goal specific priorities every day.

If you've ever been cross county skiing, you know that if you choose a popular trail, someone, probably many, have gone before you and laid down tracks. And if the snow is frozen and solid, it's very difficult to make your own unique tracks. You can have fun and get exercise, but you are stuck in the tracks of others. Sometimes life is like that. You always seem to be following in someone else's tracks. It's safer and comfortable and you can plod along without much risk of falling. But you never discover your true grit.

Forging your own path requires a brave heart. With a brave heart, you develop an opportunistic state of mind. You will live a life of design rather than default!

Promise yourself to strive for excellence in all things, even the most mundane tasks. Treat each task as importantly as the one before and after.

Ask yourself at the beginning of each day, "How can I be excellent today?" "How can I show up for myself?" And at the end of the day: "What made me happy today?" Try to find the answer in simple things and everyday tasks.

Above all, say YES to yourself.

For today, consider the assumptions you have about yourself, others, and life in light of the above list of how a proper perspective adds value to your life. I encourage you to question any assumptions that don't add value to your life. IF your assumptions are based on principles that are not subjective to changing realities, they are valid. When your assumptions are subjective to changing realities, then it's time for you to get more proactive in rewriting your inner script to live the best life for yourself.

By renewing your mind and developing productive behavior habits, you can free yourself from the mental and emotional constraints that limit the possibilities in your life. A proper perspective on life empowers you to see, think, feel, and respond to life differently. If you do something different, you will have a different experience. With different experiences, the vision and the territory of your life expand beyond the limitations to inspire greater possibilities.

Thank you for taking your time to read this book, "Deep Within." I strongly hope the information and tips provided will be helpful for you to remain self-confident no matter the obstacle and to help you develop a strong mindset which is the best way to win in this life.

Stay Fulfilled!!

www.ingramcontent.com/pod-product-compliance
Lightning Source LLC
Chambersburg PA
CBHW071415290426
44108CB00014B/1834